BEYOND SHIVA

BEYOND SHIVA

The Absolute Truth

AVAHTARA

Copyright © 2017 by Avahtara

All rights reserved. | First Edition, August 2017

The reproduction or transmission of this book in whole or in part in any manner whatsoever, including photocopying, recording, or other electronic or mechanical methods, without prior permission from the author is prohibited except in the case of brief acknowledged quotations.

ISBN: 978-1975809102

www.avahtara.com

avahtara.shiva@gmail.com

ahav|publications

This book is not meant to be used, nor should it be used, to diagnose or treat any medical condition. For diagnosis or treatment of medical problems, consult a medical professional. The author is not liable for any damage or negative consequences to any person reading or following the information in this book.

*Everything happens in its own time.
The one who is ready for
the Absolute Knowledge will be made
somehow to hear of it and follow it up.*

- Bhagavan Sri Ramana Maharshi
Talks with Sri Ramana Maharshi

Introduction

Rarely has the Absolute Truth been exposed in such a direct, profound and modern manner that goes straight into the Heart instead of the usual head.

Who is this book for?

This book is not for intellectuals.

This book is not for the faint of heart.

This book is not for those who want to dream a better dream.

This book is not for those who want to solve their mundane problems.

This book is not for those still investing in their personality.

This book IS for those who are ready for the Absolute Truth.

This book IS for those who are ready to go beyond the mind.

This book IS for those who are ready to go beyond life.

This book IS for those who are ready to go beyond themselves.

This book IS for those who are ready to go… Beyond *Shiva*!

This book goes straight into the Heart and completely dissolves the mind. The Heart is the 'placeless place' to be if you want to realize who you truly are.

This book is also not for analysis, to make logical conclusions or other mind-interpretations. Any repetition or apparent contradiction has a purpose.

You don't have to understand anything.

Understanding will always be of the mind.

Know with your Heart.

This short book is a direct pointing to yourself. Only the most profound Truth will be found here.

Feel this book with your Heart instead of reading it with your mind.

It can be read in an instant, and last a lifetime.

You may want to read each sentence slowly and stay with it, reflecting on its meaning, before proceeding to the next one. See where it is pointing at and stay there. Don't be close-minded.

Most will probably skim through this book. Then they will re-read it slowly many times. Re-reading may help you 'get it' easier.

'Getting it' simply means that what is written here takes you to yourself.

Being with yourself simply means that you stay as 'I am', as the presence of being, of existing, at the source of 'I', as empty awareness.

The more you stay like that, the more the illusion fades and the Reality shines through.

There is a chance this book will contradict most things you've heard in spirituality.

This book is not about spirituality.

It is about You.

No concepts or beliefs will be entertained.

This is only about the Absolute Truth.

This is about going beyond life itself.

Beyond the dream of creation.

Beyond God.

Beyond who you think you are into your Supreme Existence.

Beyond *Shiva*.

All the unimaginable Love, unfathomable Bliss and unshakable Peace that are dwelling inside the center of my Heart have now manifested into "Beyond Shiva: The Absolute Truth."

It is short yet infinite, a direct communication from yourself to yourself. If the Eternal Silence beyond comprehension could be put into words, this would be it.

∞

benedictory words

1.

Oh Supreme Master,
I bow before You,
humbly requesting
Your eternal blessing.

2.

Oh Supreme Master,
I salute You
for melting me into the unspeakable bliss
You unbrokenly shower upon me.

3.

Oh Supreme Reality of the Absolute
beyond words, I humbly request You,
tell me about You, tell me who or what
You Truly Are.

4.

Oh Supreme of the Supremes,
I humbly ask You to teach me,
without holding back anything,
the nature of the Absolute Truth.

∞

I. Shiva

1.

A Teacher will teach you.

A Master will awake you.

I will destroy you.

2.

The Truth destroys.

Destroys the lie forever.

The lie that never existed.

3.

Because I am *Shiva*.

I am the Auspicious One.

I am the Truth.

∞

2. liberation

1.

I am not bound, nor am I liberated.

I am not enlightened, nor am I ignorant.

'I', I am not.

There is no 'I' in Me.

There is no 'me' in I.

No 'I' has ever come to Me.

No 'I' has ever presented itself to Me.

2.

No 'I' have I ever seen.

No 'other' have I ever seen.

'I' implies 'other'.

'Other' implies 'I'.

There are no 'I' and no 'other' in Me.

There is even no 'me' in Me.

There is even no 'I' in I.

I am beyond 'I', 'me' and 'other'.

I am beyond concepts and experiences.

I am beyond beyond-ness.

3.

Don't read what is written.

Feel what is written.

I am not pointing at myself.

There is no 'myself' in I.

There is no 'I' in Myself.

I am pointing at yourself-less Self.

I am pointing at your I-less Self.

4.

Liberation is a play in the illusion of bondage.

Liberation is created by bondage.

Remove the one who has to get liberated and there is no bondage.

Moksha, Salvation, *Nirvana*, Liberation, Self-Realization, *Sat-Chit-Ananda*, Freedom, *Jnana*, Enlightenment, *Manonasa*, and so on, are only concepts.

What do they mean to you?

They have significance because you believe you are bound.

They have significance because you believe you are ignorant.

Remove the one who believes.

Remove that 'I' and you will truly See.

5.

Feel your sense of existence.

Feel your 'I am'.

Feel your 'I exist'.

Feel the source of your 'I'.

They are all false.

But so are you.

A false you, staying in the illusory sense of presence, getting illusionary liberation from a false illusion.

6.

Then you will forget.

Then you won't remember.

Then you won't be you.

You will know that you never needed to get liberated because you were never bound.

But this is false.

You will not even know that you never needed to get liberated from an illusion.

You will not know anything.

Not knowing anything is not ignorance.

It is the Supreme blissful wisdomless wisdom.

You-less you.

That which remains.

∞

3. Existence

1.

You don't exist.

The others don't exist.

The world doesn't exist.

The universe doesn't exist.

Nor even I exist.

I am a product of your mind.

Your mind can't conceive Me, for the Limitless can't be understood by the limited, the Infinite can't be understood by the finite.

The mind will always conceptualize the conceptless and superimpose the illusion of 'I' on the I-less illusionless.

2.

In deep sleep you don't exist.

In deep sleep others don't exist.

In deep sleep the world doesn't exist.

In deep sleep the universe doesn't exist.

In deep sleep the 'I' you believe I am doesn't exist.

3.

Yet something is aware that there was nothing during deep dreamless sleep.

How can you possibly know there was a period of nothingness, no experience, no phenomenon, no objects, just nothing, during deep dreamless sleep?

Because there is awareness.

If there was no awareness, you wouldn't know you had that dreamless sleeping period.

You would go from the waking-state-frame directly to the dreaming-state-frame and back to the waking-state-frame without periods of nothingness in between.

However, even this witness awareness is only known after your mind has risen yet again in the waking state.

4.

There is no witness during deep sleep.

There is knowledge of the witnessing of deep sleep in the waking state.

The witness of deep sleep is, therefore, knowledge of the mind.

The witness of deep sleep is, therefore, a creation of the mind.

It is the mind trying to conceive the Absolute.

5.

The mind can't conceive non-duality.

The mind can't conceive the Absolute.

The mind distorts deep sleep into a duality state by creating the illusory knowledge of a witness of the absence of everything.

The mind is a big liar.

There is no end to the mind's questions and problems.

It is the experience of everyone that there is no witness during deep sleep.

The witnessing of deep sleep is a marvelous illusion that made even great Sages concede ignorance about a supposed 'causal body' to those unable to accept the Absolute Truth.

The 'causal body' is nothing but a delusion created by the mind.

6.

The mind itself is an illusion, an erroneous awareness of yourself.

The witness of deep sleep is also an illusion.

Deep sleep is a concept created by the mind.

There are no concepts in deep sleep.

There is no mind in deep sleep.

There is no witness during deep sleep.

There is no unconsciousness in deep sleep.

There is unconsciousness in deep sleep for the mind.

The mind creates all sorts of theories, concepts, reasons, illustrations, and logic.

The mind is a concept sustained by concepts.

There is no such thing as the mind.

7.

Find your mind.

Right now.

Try to find it.

Only emptiness will pervade.

8.

Emptiness is not the Absolute Truth.

Emptiness is a concept.

Emptiness only survives on the dualistic notion of fullness.

Empty of objects, full of objects.

Such is the nature of the mind.

9.

Yet mind created no-mind.

No-mind is a concept.

There is no no-mind in no-mind.

There is no-mind in mind.

10.

The mind comes from the darkness of nothingness.

Every morning, when you wake up or even dream, there comes the rising of the mind from the darkness of nothingness.

This nothingness is just ignorance of oneself.

It is due to this ignorance that everything can spring forth.

11.

There has to be darkness in a cinema room so that the multiplicity of images can be projected onto the screen.

On a truly illuminated room, no projected image can be seen.

This darkness is ignorance of who you are.

This ignorance allows the mind to rise up.

Lights off and experiencing nothingness is the knowledge the mind has of deep sleep after it has awakened up.

12.

This mind is nothing but an erroneous and impure awareness of who you are.

Because of this mind, you think 'I am x-y-z'.

Remove the 'x-y-z' and stay exclusively on the 'I am'.

Stay as 'I am'.

Dwell as 'I am'.

Be as I am.

Put some Light on this darkness of ignorance.

Let the Light on, all the time.

The Light is now never turned off.

Actually, there was never darkness.

The Light was never off, it just appeared to be.

13.

Stay with the 'I am' until there is no more 'I' to be.

Then, and only then, will you Truly Exist.

But not you who you take yourself to be.

You-less you.

Existence beyond the concept of existence.

Beyond existence.

Beyond beyond-ness.

∞

4. here and now

1.

I am not here.

I am nowhere to be found.

I am beyond the so called here-ness.

Tell Me, is there a 'here' in deep sleep?

The 'here' is a creation of the mind.

2.

I am not now.

I am nowhere to be found.

Tell Me, is there a 'now' in deep sleep?

The 'now' is a creation of the mind.

I am not now, not here, I am not nowhere.

I am beyond the mind, I am beyond concepts, I am beyond experiences, I am beyond all three.

3.

The 'here' and 'now' can be useful.

Here and now feel your presence.

Here and now feel your sense of existence.

Here and now look for the looker.

Here and now know the knower.

Here and now seek the seeker.

Here and now see the seer.

Here and now observe the observer.

Here and now be aware of existing.

Here and now be aware of being conscious.

Here and now feel the 'I am'.

Here and now stay as 'I am'.

Here and now love the 'I am'.

Here and now stay at the source of your 'I'.

Here and now stay as awareness.

Here and now love your awareness.

Here and now melt the background and the foreground by dissolving into the Heart.

Here and now let go.

Here and now stay in that emptiness.

Here and now stay in that stillness.

Here and now stay in that joy.

Here and now stay in that silence.

Here and now stay in that bliss.

Here and now stay in that love.

Here and now stay in that happiness.

Here and now stay in that aliveness.

Here and now stay in that awareness.

Here and now stay in that voidness.

Here and now stay in that nothingness.

Here and now stay in that peace.

Here and now stay as That.

4.

This is all done in the realm of space-time.

Your illusion is in space-time.

The mind is in space-time.

You have to break the illusion by walking an illusory path.

Why does it matter if the Self is perfect, everlasting, ever-attained, and so on?

Those are just concepts for you until you end the illusion of being someone.

The illusory illusion must be slain by the illusory sword of self-abidance.

5.

Be nothing.

Being nothing is freedom.

Being nothing is true joy.

Be nothing.

6.

It doesn't matter if it doesn't make sense.

Making sense is mind.

Making no sense is mind.

Being beyond the need of making sense or beyond the worry of not making any sense is where you have to be.

7.

Just trust.

Just surrender.

Just abide in yourself.

Just be self-aware.

Just be.

∞

5. all is one

1.

The most beautiful dance ever performed by *Maya*.

The most beautiful song ever sang by *Maya*.

The most beautiful of the lies ever told by *Maya*.

2.

'All is One' is *Maya*.

'All' is a product of the mind.

'All' being 'One' is a knowledge of the mind.

There is no 'All' nor 'One' in deep dreamless sleep.

3.

Again, dancing with concepts you are.

Again, dancing with experiences you are.

All experiences are created by the mind.

The mind doesn't exist.

4.

'All is One' is the ultimate illusion.

Who are you that knows 'All'
and knows 'One'?

You surely love duality.

You surely love *Maya*.

5.

In both the dream that you call real life,
and the dream that you dream at night,
you can have such an illusory experience.

The experience of everything being One.

The differences between the dreaming and waking state are like a mirage.

6.

"Whenever I look, I see *Brahman*."

— you say.

"Whatever I perceive is the Self."

— you say.

"Everything is Consciousness."

— you say.

7.

Isn't everything the mind?

When you wake up in the morning, the world appears.

When you go out sleep at night,
the world disappears.

8.

Isn't this your experience?

Why do you say 'everything is One'?

'Everything is One' is true in the sense that everything is the mind.

When the mind rises, everything rises.

When the mind subsides, everything subsides.

9.

I stay eternally untouched by that.

I am not even aware of such fluctuations.

Everything comes from the mind.

The mind is the true substance of all things.

10.

I am beyond the mind.

I am beyond everything.

There are no 'things' in Me.

There is no 'All' in Me.

There is no 'One' in Me.

I am beyond multiplicity or unicity.

That is all mind.

That is all *Maya*.

11.

I stay timelessly in peace beyond peace.

I stay timelessly in love beyond love.

I stay timelessly in bliss beyond bliss.

I stay timelessly in silence beyond silence.

I stay timelessly in beyond-ness beyond beyond-ness.

∞

6. Creation

1.

You are the creator of everythingness.

You are the creator of all things.

You, mind, are a wonderful thing.

You, *Maya*, are a marvelous thing.

You, *Maya*, are a majestic creator.

Your masterpiece, this living universe, is indeed sublime.

2.

But has creation ever taken place in Me?

Has the universe ever been created and dissolved?

Has the cycle of birth and death of the universe and everything in it ever appeared in Me?

Have I ever been aware of the universe?

Have I ever been aware of Creation?

Have I ever been aware of Dissolution?

3.

Where was the creation of your last night's dream?

Where was the dissolution of your last night's dream?

Where did your dream happen?

It just appeared from nothing.

It just disappeared into nothing.

The mind just created it out of nothing.

The mind dissolved it into nothing.

I have nothing to do with it.

4.

In deep sleep there is no talk about creation.

In deep sleep there is no talk about dissolution.

In deep sleep there is no talk about the universe.

In deep sleep there is no mind.

5.

No mind means no creation.

No mind doesn't mean the voice in your head stopped.

No mind doesn't mean thoughtlessness.

No mind doesn't mean 'impersonal presence'.

No mind means inconceivable and unqualified non-dual Bliss alone.

Bliss beyond bliss.

6.

Creation is a product of the mind.

The pure mind says she just borrowed My light.

The pure mind is like the Sun's reflection on the Moon.

The Moon has no light of its own.

Only the Sun is luminous.

7.

The impure mind thinks it is self-luminous.

The impure mind is the source of separation.

The impure mind is the source of misery.

The impure mind is the source of opposites.

The impure mind is a terrible thing for you.

The impure mind is indeed inglorious.

8.

The pure mind knows it is not self-luminous.

The pure mind is happy.

The pure mind is sapient.

Make your mind pure by hearing My words.

A time will come when you are ready for the Absolute Truth.

Then you shall stop reading these words.

You will simply dissolve your pure mind and know:

Nothing ever emanated from Me.

9.

I am not the creator of anything.

I have never created anything.

I am not the substratum of everything because nothing besides Me truly exists.

10.

You are no other than *Shiva*.

You are no other than I.

You are not a creator.

You are not *Maya*.

You without you are the Absolute Awareness.

You-less you is the Truth.

11.

Is this too much to the illusory impure mind?

May your non-existing mind explode into the lightless light of the ever-and-only beyond-existence Absolute Auspicious One.

∞

7. Maya

1.

Maya is beautiful.

Maya is horrible.

Maya is happiness.

Maya is misery.

Maya is peace.

Maya is agitation.

Maya is duality.

2.

One thing doesn't come without its opposite.

Finding true happiness in *Maya* is indeed impossible.

Finding everlasting happiness in *Maya* is indeed impossible.

Happiness in *Maya* is simply a short rest between the end and the beginning of sorrow.

3.

In deep sleep, from the perspective of the mind, there is still ignorance.

In deep sleep, it is the experience of everyone that there is no time nor space.

From *Maya*, the primary ignorance, did time and space come.

Upon the rising of the mind, in a sleeping-dream or on the waking-dream, did time and space come.

Time and space come from the ignorance of oneself.

4.

Maya has no beginning.

Maya has no cause.

Maya has no origin.

Maya is ignorance.

5.

Tell me, what is the cause of *Maya*?

Tell me, what is the origin of *Maya*?

Many shall say it is the Absolute.

Many shall say it is the Self.

Many shall say it is Pure Awareness.

Many shall say it is Me.

Many shall say I decided to experience.

Many shall say I decided to taste duality.

Many shall say I and *Maya* are One.

Many shall say *Maya* is I, manifested.

6.

'Many' is equal to *Maya*.

Maya is equal to 'Many'.

Maya has no cause because *Maya* doesn't exist.

Ignorance has no origin because ignorance doesn't exist.

Ignorance never had a beginning.

Ignorance never existed.

Ignorance doesn't exist.

Ignorance will never exist.

There is no ignorance in Me.

There is nothing apart from Me.

Only the Absolute Truth truly Exists.

7.

No desire to experience has ever arisen in Me.

No desire to taste duality has ever arisen in Me.

Nothing has even arisen in Me.

No veil has ever covered Me.

8.

I was never born.

I am beyond unborn-ness.

The Truth simply Is.

9.

Some say the Enlightened being perceives the world.

Some say the Enlightened being is not aware of the world.

They are talking about different things.

10.

The world is an illusion created by the mind.

The world is perceivable through the five senses.

The five senses are part of the mind.

What perceives the world is the mind.

Without mind, there is no world.

What doesn't perceive the world, because
no world nor mind has ever existed,
exists or will ever exist, is the Absolute.

11.

The one who is lucid is still dreaming.

He is happy.

He knows emotions come and go.

He knows thoughts come and go.

He doesn't get affected by them.

His I-ness doesn't bind him.

It is like a burnt rope.

It cannot cause bondage.

He knows the source of everything
is One.

He can also know the source of everything is the mind.

He can also know the source of the mind is the darkness of ignorance.

But he has yet to go past it.

He might not know that.

The one who is lucid is not awake.

He is still dreaming the dream, although more lucidly than before.

12.

The one who is awake is not dreaming.

The dream has ended.

Nothing is perceivable because 'no-thing' exists to be perceived.

When you awake from a dream, the dream ends.

13.

The mind will always perceive the world.

The ignorant mind thinks
"I am the body."

The enlightened mind knows Pure Awareness to be its True Nature.

The enlightened mind has switched its identification from "I am the body" to "I am Pure Awareness."

Yet that enlightened mind will still perceive the world.

The world will always be dualistic.

The mind will always be dualistic.

14.

The ignorant mind is like the Moon that looks at the planet Earth and believes itself to be self-luminous.

The lucid mind is like the Moon that looks at the planet Earth but knows its light to be from the Sun.

The enlightened mind is like the Moon that looks at the Sun and knows its light to be from the Sun.

The Sun stays ever unaffected, ever the same, absolutely unconcerned with anything whatsoever.

The true Enlightened being is like the Sun.

Yet, to the perspective of others, while his body lasts, he will be like the Moon, but an Enlightened Moon.

15.

The mind can be so engrossed in the Light of Awareness that it dissolves itself into pure Ecstasy.

Only the mind can get liberated from the wrong notion it has of itself.

Pure Awareness never changes.

16.

Don't analyze with your head these words.

They are just pointers.

Pure Awareness is not an object nor can be looked at by the mind.

These are just examples to help you understand.

They are not the Absolute Truth.

17.

I don't perceive the world because the world is only perceivable by the mind.

I am beyond the mind.

I have no knowledge of the world whatsoever.

I have no knowledge of anything at all.

I have not even written these words.

Nobody has written them.

I stand as I am.

I simply am.

I without I simply Am beyond Am-ness.

The Truth simply Is.

∞

8. Who am I?

1.

I am not a being.

I am not blue.

I am not any color.

I am not male.

I am not female.

I am not an entity.

I am not with a form.

I am not from any religion.

I am not from any tradition.

I am not a concept.

I am not imagined.

I am not visible.

I am not invisible.

I am not real.

I am not unreal.

I am not from the Himalayas.

I am not from anywhere in the world.

I am not everything.

I am not nothing.

I am not like the cloudless sky.

I am not like space.

I am not energy.

I am not a witness.

I am not the eternal subject.

I am not that which is aware of other things.

I am not that which is aware of the presence of everythingness.

I am not that which is aware of the absence of everythingness.

I am not nothingness.

I am not a void.

I am not emptiness.

I am not fullness.

I am not universal consciousness.

I am not cosmic consciousness.

2.

I am not anything you can conceive.

I am not anything you can write.

I am not anything you can speak.

I am not anything you can hear.

I am not anything you can smell.

I am not anything you can touch.

I am not anything you can taste.

I am not anything you can see.

I am not anything you can sense.

I am not anything you can feel.

I am not anything you can think.

I am not anything you can perceive.

I am not anything you can imagine.

I am not anything you can experience.

I am not anything you can dream.

I am not anything you can express.

3.

They say I am God.

They say I am indivisible.

They say I am immutable.

They say I am peace.

They say I am love.

They say I am bliss.

They say I am happiness.

They say I am joy.

They say I am silence.

They say I am eternal.

They say I am infinite.

They say I am the Supreme Being.

They say I am non-Being.

They say I am a mystery.

They say I am non-duality.

They say I am formless.

They say I am like the light of a million suns.

They say I am unmanifested.

They say I am unborn.

They say I am *Brahman*.

They say I am *ParaBrahman*.

They say I am the Self.

They say I am pure Awareness.

They say I am the Absolute.

They say I am *Shiva*.

4.

I am beyond God.

I am beyond indivisibleness.

I am beyond immutableness.

I am beyond peace.

I am beyond love.

I am beyond bliss.

I am beyond happiness.

I am beyond joy.

I am beyond silence.

I am beyond eternity.

I am beyond infinity.

I am beyond the Supreme Being.

I am beyond non-Being.

I am beyond any mystery.

I am beyond non-duality.

I am beyond being formless.

I am beyond the light of a million suns.

I am beyond the unmanifested.

I am beyond being unborn.

I am beyond *Brahman*.

I am beyond *ParaBrahman*.

5.

These are all just concepts.

These are all just words.

I am That which concepts shall never ever describe.

I am That which words shall never ever describe.

I am beyond concepts.

I am beyond words.

I am beyond beyond-ness.

6.

I am beyond the Self.

I am the Self beyond the concept of the Self.

The Self is just a concept created by the ego-self.

7.

I am beyond pure Awareness.

I am pure Awareness beyond the concept of pure Awareness.

Pure Awareness is just a concept created by impure awareness.

8.

I am beyond the Absolute.

I am the Absolute beyond the concept of the Absolute.

Absolute is just a concept created by the relative.

9.

I am beyond *Shiva*.

I am *Shiva* beyond the concept of *Shiva*.

Shiva is just a concept created by *jiva*.

10.

I am *Shiva* beyond *Shiva*.

You are *Shiva* beyond *Shiva*.

Shiva is *Shiva* beyond *Shiva*.

That is the Absolute Truth.

∞

If this book has touched your Heart, please support the author by leaving a review.

Read also by the same author:

"Conversations with the Truth"

Available as Kindle and Paperback at Amazon.

Visit the website to download
Free eBooks by Avahtara:

www.avahtara.com

You can join our the Facebook Group by clicking on 'Facebook Group' on the website's menu.

If you have any questions, doubts, want clarification on some passages or would like to get more teachings, you can contact the author at:

avahtara.shiva@gmail.com

Glossary

Brahman

Name used in *Sanātana Dharma* (Hinduism) for the Absolute, the Self or the Ultimate Reality, while for others, it might represent *Ishvara* instead, God with form, the totality of mind or the ruler of the universe (they use *Para-Brahman* for the Absolute).

Jiva

Individual being.

Maya

The illusion of Creation, the primary ignorance of who you Truly Are. In its pristine 'form-less form' it is the Darkness of Nothingness.

Moksha, Nirvana, Manonasa, Jnana

Synonyms for Liberation, Enlightenment and so on.

ParaBrahman

The Absolute. It is the same as *Advaita Vedanta*'s Brahman.

Sat-Chit-Ananda

Existence-Awareness-Bliss.

Shiva

Who or what you Truly Are. Completely beyond description. What this book points towards.

Contents

Introduction 9

Benedictory Words......................19

1. Shiva 23

2. Liberation 25

3. Existence 33

4. Here and Now 45

5. All is One.........................53

6. Creation 61

7. Maya 69

8. Who am I?.........................83

Glossary 96

Printed in Great Britain
by Amazon